Dubai

DISCOVERED

EXPLORER
www.explorerpublishing.com

Front cover photograph
Madinat Jumeirah & Burj Al Arab

Back cover photograph
Dubai Creek Golf & Yacht Club Marina

Photography
Victor Romero

Text
David Quinn & Joseph Rowland

Dubai Discovered
1st Edition September 2005
Reprint May 2008

Published By
Explorer Publishing & Distribution
PO Box 34275, Dubai, UAE
Phone (+971-4) 340 8805
Fax (+971-4) 340 8806
Email: info@explorerpublishing.com

978-9948-442-69-1

Design – Explorer Designlab
Printing – Emirates Printing Press

DISCOVERED

DISCOVERING DUBAI

With a vista of sky-scraping sculptures and out-of-this-world hotels it is hard to imagine that little more than 50 years ago Dubai's desert skyline was vastly undiscovered. While traders from the four corners of the world may have found their way to the flourishing trading port at the creek, bringing with them a myriad of influences from the Middle East and beyond, there was little other reason to visit this small, insignificant stretch of coastland. Fast forward to 21st century Dubai and every frame of today's picture is radically different. As you will see from this collection of awe-inspiring images, Dubai has become a city of contrasts, an oasis of opportunity and a destination to discover. The remarkable evolution of one of the world's most intriguing modern metropolises makes Dubai not just another location on the tourist map, but rather an unprecedented sanctuary where cultures collide in unopposed harmony.

What makes Dubai so unique is the fact that traditions of the Middle East not only meet but also mix with the futuristic facets of the modern west. Nowhere is this more evident than at the heart of Dubai, the instrumental creek. Here wooden dhows continue to trade their plethora of produce, from fresh vegetables to the latest electronics, against a backdrop of shining skyscrapers, where cross-cultural business deals are made by the dozen. Visitors can witness this congruous exchange by floating down the creek on an abra (wooden water taxi), then disembarking at the Deira side where the souks (local markets) entice with mesmerising gold and tantalising spices.

A stroll through the souks is just one of the many discoveries that make every experience of Dubai an unforgettable memory. Another striking impression is the iconic Burj Al Arab. Recognised instantly around the world, this inspirational hotel rises out of the azure waters of the Arabian Gulf and stands for the vision, determination and exquisite hospitality of this celebrated emirate. Following in such tall-order footsteps is the Palm Jumeirah, where fronds stretch into the sea and play host to luxury living. The fact that it can be seen from space with the naked eye provides another example of the inconceivable becoming credible in this creative paradise where imagination is embraced and dreams become reality. Two more palms and a cluster of man-made islands arranged in the shape of the world map further convey Dubai's resolve to develop without limitations and beyond boundaries.

Dubai's transformation may have bred from its creek and coastal trading access but the true catalyst for this city's metamorphosis came from beneath the water's surface, where the discovery of expansive oil reserves changed history. Some may have thought that this massive influx of wealth may have led to jaded traditional cultures but, on the contrary, financial stability has helped to bridge the gap between this corner of Arabia and the rest of the world. While modernity has made its mark in record-breaking beachfront hotels and creekside corporate towers, traditional life in Dubai remains steadfast. Visitors can bear witness to its living history in the old area of Bastakiya where windtowers pay homage to a bygone era and the Dubai Museum pays tribute to a heritage that continues to govern modern life. The Jumeira Mosque stands equally proud amongst its glittering hotel neighbours, signifying the strength of tradition and inviting visitors to gain a greater understanding of the Islamic faith. With its arms open as a growing trading port Dubai has remained welcoming, accessible and culturally diverse – be it in the eclectic mix of architectural works of art that bless the horizon, in the cacophony of cuisines that populate many a hotel menu, or in the mixed bag of nationalities that grace the city's shores.

A drive down Sheikh Zayed Road, Dubai's main highway bordered by an unregimented row of individually inspired buildings (captained by the splendid Emirates Towers, and watched over by the cloud-busting Burj Dubai, now the world's tallest building), leaves visitors with no doubt as to why Dubai receives such international respect. As the rest of the world has discovered the treasures of this Arabian gem over the last half century, global events too have found their way to its unrivalled stage. The Dubai Desert Classic golf tournament, the Dubai Tennis Championships and the world's richest horse race, the Dubai World Cup, are all testament to the emirate's burgeoning appeal. Visitors flock to Dubai's playground not only to witness sport history in the making but also to enjoy the vast range of activities on offer, including desert driving, paragliding and a host of watersports. Not to be overshadowed by sport, the shopping is equally renowned. There are the various first-class shopping malls that take on a life of their own during the annual shopping festival in winter, the interesting souks that beg for some bargaining and the numerous boutiques that entice the biggest of spenders. Complementing the cosmopolitan collection of shopping opportunities is the gastronomic selection of restaurants, bars and nightclubs that leave no appetite unsatisfied.

The following pages come alive with the spirit and adventure of Dubai. While life may have changed dramatically and landscapes have developed beyond recognition, the essence of this desert retreat remains the same. From the breathtaking mountains of Hatta and the eerie silence of the arresting desert to the natural draw of the creek and the elegant flamingos that have found sanctuary at its head, Dubai deserves to be discovered time and time again.

DUBAI THEN

There is a common tendency to divide the history of Dubai, and by extension the Emirates, into pre- and post-oil days. While the distinction is in many ways valid, a closer look at Dubai's development and rich history reveals several monumental developments before the discovery of oil that were instrumental in Dubai's getting to where it is today. Most notable among these factors are a people's uncanny ability to adapt to their environment, a fortuitous geographical location and, possibly more than anything else, an astounding run of stable and visionary leadership which has proactively guided the emirate into its position as one of today's global hotspots.

Early inhabitants of the area that is now known as Dubai were faced with the challenge of thriving in the difficult and limited choices of geography with which they were presented. Notwithstanding daytime temperatures regularly reaching over 40°C, the vast deserts could not have provided a great deal of sustenance due to an extreme lack of water, yet tribes of Bedouin moved across the land, raising goats and camels, and cultivating dates through ingenious irrigation systems known as falaj, which are still used in a similar fashion today. Similarly, the mountainous regions to the north and east of today's city were, if not inhospitable, an astoundingly difficult place to live. Nevertheless, early farmers created networks of trails while herding goats and developing rudimentary farms and settlements.

Similarly lacking natural resources, inhabitants of the coastal areas took to the sea to support themselves, thriving from fishing and later pearling and sea trade. It is this development more than any other that has led to Dubai's modern situation as a worldwide hub of trade and transport.

For early settlers from the Bani Yas tribe, the natural inlet that is now known as the creek provided a safe port and natural haven for trading with other tribes of the region. However, archaeological findings suggest that trading caravans were coming through the region as early as the seventh century AD, meaning that by the time the Bani Yas arrived in the early 1800s, the region had been part of an extensive trading network for centuries. It had attracted the attention of both the Portuguese and the British, who tried with varying degrees of success to control the trade routes and stifle piracy.

The Bani Yas, however, had the good fortune of being led by Maktoum bin Butti, who began a long tradition of tax exemption for traders, and whose ancestors wisely entered into exclusive (and lucrative) contracts with the British. As a result of these dealings, merchants from previous trading centres in Sharjah and Persia relocated to Dubai, setting the stage for the multi-cultural city that stands today, and establishing Dubai as the pre-eminent trading centre in the Gulf region.

As the pearling industry fell into a slow decline in the early part of the 20th century, the ruling family depended more and more on trade as a means of promoting Dubai and supporting its economy.

By some estimates, the population of Dubai had risen to nearly 20,000 people by the beginning of the second world war – a small town compared to today's bustling city, but an impressive number in those pre-air-conditioning days, especially considering that nearly a quarter of the population was expatriate. A brave decision by Sheikh Rashid bin Saeed Al Maktoum, the ruler at the time, would cause both a boom in the local population and construction, while setting a precedent of bold innovation which would be a hallmark of Dubai's development to the present day. As trade traffic using the creek increased in the late 1950s, a steady accumulation of silt and natural erosion began to make the creek difficult, if not impossible, to navigate. Seeing the potential crisis, Sheikh Rashid made the financially costly, yet highly foresighted, decision to dredge and widen the creek, thereby expanding its capacity to handle more and larger ships. With this, Dubai became the *de facto* trading centre of the Middle East, creating a need for increased port facilities, including what at the time was the substantial Port Rashid.

In the early 1970s Sheikh Rashid began formulating the idea for a massive port to be built at Jebel Ali. Again, the idea at the time seemed nearly impossible. Similarly grand in scale were the Dubai Dry Docks. History has of course proven the success of these endeavours again and again. Perhaps more visionary, however, was the formation of the Jebel Ali Free Zone around the Jebel Ali Port. Taking a cue from his grandfather, Sheikh Maktoum bin Hasher, who in 1901 set the stage for Dubai's duty-free future, Sheikh Rashid established the port as a major trade zone through designation of the free zone, eventually leading to its becoming the largest shipping destination in the Gulf.

These latter developments were of course financed by the discovery of oil in 1966, shortly after the completion of the creek expansion project, which greatly increased their scale and the speed at which they could be constructed. However, it is essential to recognise the enormity of these tasks and the potential failure inherent in each of them, which was not lost on many of Sheikh Rashid's closest advisors. The discovery of oil has undoubtedly changed the lifestyle of the average Emirati citizen greatly, and has upped the ante, so to speak, on development for the city. Yet the successful application of these funds has been a testament to the unparalleled vision of its leaders, continuing into today's sometimes bewildering developments.

DUBAI NOW

The late ruler of Dubai, His Highness Sheikh Rashid bin Saeed Al Maktoum, was very wise in his utilisation of the riches created by the sudden discovery of oil. It allowed for the development of an economic and social infrastructure that is the basis of today's modern society. He also had the foresight to realise that oil, and the wealth it brought, wouldn't last forever, and so alternative sources of revenue would be required. Measures to diversify the economy were quickly implemented, and as a result Dubai now has one of the world's fastest growing economies, and one that is increasingly fuelled by the trade, manufacturing and service industries. The growth of non-oil sectors has allowed Dubai to reduce its dependency on oil to less than 6% of its gross domestic product, a figure that is falling every year. It is estimated that by 2010, oil will contribute just 1% to the annual GDP.

Dubai was founded on trade, and this remains the biggest contributor to the city's wealth. The Jebel Ali Free Zone is home to thousands of companies who take advantage of Dubai's strategic location in the Gulf, and its gateway position between east and west. The main businesses are manufacturing, warehousing and distribution, with companies enjoying 100% duty exemption on goods imported for re-export. The free zone is built around the world's largest man-made port, and covers over 100 square kilometres. Of course, the historically important Dubai Creek still plays an important role in trade, and at any time fully loaded dhows can be seen navigating into the heart of the city to unload cargo.

As well as being an important trading centre, Dubai is also emerging as the regional hub for corporate financial activities. The Dubai International Financial Centre attracts international investors with state-of-the-art facilities and a zero tax rate, and the intention is to match the financial centres of London, New York and Hong Kong.

Further investment in modern industries can be seen in projects such as Media City and Internet City. Media City has rapidly become a regional hub for local and international broadcasters, publishers and media professionals, while Internet City is home to the major names in the IT industry. Future plans are no less impressive. Business Bay will be a new commercial environment built around an extension of the creek, and Dubai Silicon Oasis will be a technology park for design and manufacturing firms in the micro-electronics and semi-conductor industries. The phenomenal success of these, and other such initiatives, can be put down to their 'free zone' status, with 100% foreign ownership, exemption of taxes and customs duties, and the benefit of streamlined bureaucracy.

Perhaps the most obvious example of Dubai's ongoing growth is the amount of construction that can be seen throughout the city. The construction industry itself is an increasingly important contributor to the city's strong economy. A new, multi-billion dollar project seems to be announced daily, each one more ambitious than the last. These projects are creating hundreds of new residential, leisure and entertainment developments aimed at increasing both the residential population and the number of tourists visiting Dubai. The most high-profile projects, publicised worldwide and now familiar to millions, include the three Palm Islands and the Burj Dubai; but there are other, equally ambitious projects scheduled for completion in the near future. All construction limitations are being challenged – for the Palm Islands and 'The World', contractors have reclaimed vast portions of land for development into luxurious residential and leisure areas.

Undoubtedly the biggest project currently underway is Dubailand. Occupying a huge area of desert to the south-east of the city, Dubailand will comprise six separate themed worlds – Attractions & Experience World, Retail & Entertainment World, Themed Leisure & Vacation World, Eco Tourism World, Sports & Outdoor World, and the 'Downtown' area. Among the many attractions, the project will feature three full-size sports stadiums, a ski resort (with real snow), over 50 hotels, the world's largest shopping mall, a nature reserve, and the already completed Dubai Autodrome. The scale is actually difficult to comprehend but, put simply, when completed this will be the biggest leisure, entertainment and retail destination on the planet, and should help Dubai achieve its target of attracting 15 million tourists a year by 2010.

To keep pace with the huge growth in resident and visitor numbers, the city is also embarking on a scheme to improve its transport network. Dubai International Airport has seen a massive expansion in recent years, including the construction of a new Terminal Three exclusively for Emirates Airline. The airport is ranked as one of the fastest growing in the world. Announced in 2005, a brand new airport at Jebel Ali will provide further options for travellers. To alleviate the pressure on Dubai's roads, an ambitious metro project will link various areas of the city by a modern rail network – the first phase is scheduled for completion by 2009.

Dubai has transformed almost beyond recognition in such a short amount of time, and given the developments that are planned or currently underway the city is set to continue growing and evolving into a truly 21st century city. A visit to Dubai is a rare opportunity, in such a modern and developed world, to witness history in the making.

The modern steel and glass skyscrapers on either side of Sheikh Zayed Road are a reminder of how Dubai has grown – quite literally – from the small coastal town it was just a generation ago. The Emirates Towers, with their impressive height and distinctive yet simple style, are perhaps the most recognisable structures lining Dubai's main highway, but each new building adds its own unique and ambitious stamp to this instantly recognisable skyline.

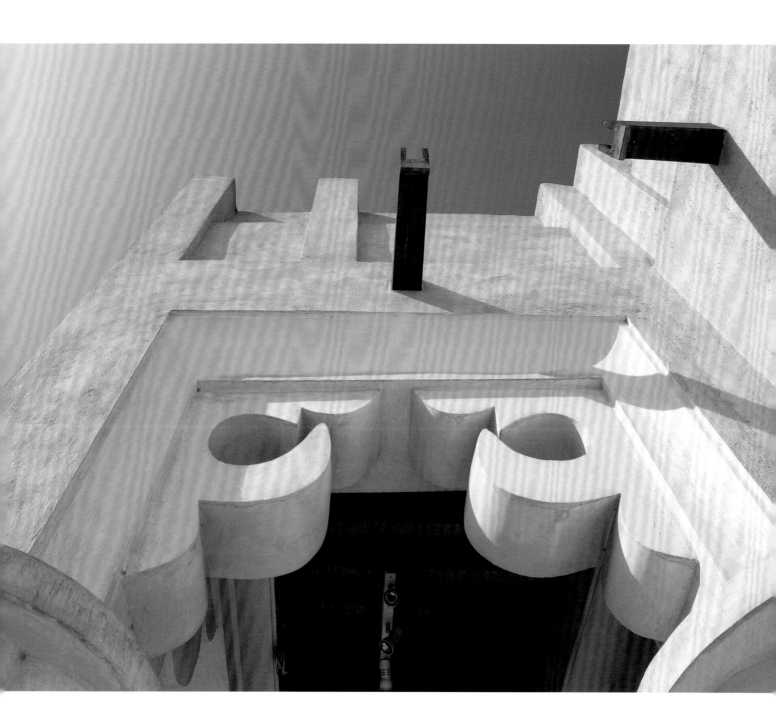

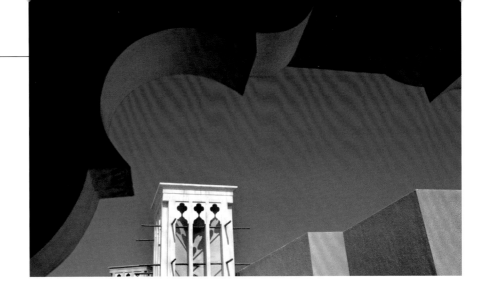

In the early 1900s, Dubai's ruler encouraged Persian merchants (predominantly from the Bastak area in southern Iran) to settle along the creek with the offer of tax concessions and free land. And so developed the bustling, historical Bastakiya area. Characterised by narrow, winding alleyways, secluded courtyards and old houses (many of which have been converted into cafés, art galleries and museums), this is an area that invites exploration. The architecture features traditional windows, ornate wooden doors and intricately detailed arches, but perhaps the most notable sight is the rectangular windtowers perched on the rooftops – the earliest form of air conditioning.

You may have seen the pictures, but nothing can prepare you for the scale and beauty of Dubai's most famous landmark when you finally see it with your own eyes. Resembling a billowing sail, the Burj Al Arab ('tower of the Arabs') stands at 321 metres and is the world's tallest hotel. The ultimate in opulence and luxury, it really is a hotel fit for kings, queens and sheikhs.

Reflecting the region's nautical history, the design of the Dubai Creek Golf and Yacht Club clubhouse echoes the sails of a traditional dhow and has become a well-known landmark in the city. The club features both an 18 hole championship course and a nine-hole course (floodlit for when the sun goes down), while the adjacent marina provides mooring for yachts of all sizes – the perfect base from which to cruise the creek or far beyond. And after a tough day on the greens or at the helm, weary golfers and skippers can unwind at one of the many bars and fine-dining restaurants.

Traditional Arabic architecture, while stately and efficient, can often be less ornate than other styles. At the same time, decorative flourishes such as intricately carved doors add a functional beauty while also illustrating the measure to which Arabs value their privacy and security. These heavy wooden doors, often with elaborate geometric or floral designs, and sometimes large brass spikes for added strength, can still be seen adorning houses in some of Dubai's older districts such as Bastakiya.

Dubai has some of the world's most opulent hotels located within its city limits, and endless desert beyond, so it was only a matter of time before someone combined the two to create a luxury desert resort. Bab Al Shams ('Gateway to the Sun') has been designed in a traditional fort setting and is home to the region's first authentic open-air Arabic desert restaurant. The resort has a kids' club, health and leisure facilities including the luxurious Satori Spa, and a swimming pool and bar offering breathtaking views over the dunes.

It's surprising to see the unmistakable outline of flamingos wading peacefully in the waters of the Ras Al Khor Wildlife Sanctuary, which is surrounded by a busy road network and at the end of Dubai Creek. An important feeding ground and roosting site, the sanctuary attracts up to 30,000 birds of varying species. Watchtowers have been built allowing visitors to get close to the birds without disturbing them, and there are telescopes and binoculars provided – a welcome sign of Dubai's growing commitment to ecotourism.

New Dubai was once considered something of an outpost. These days, the area seems to be home to virtually all the city's hottest spots, and one of the coolest ones – the Middle East's first indoor ski resort, with five different runs and a fully fledged ski school.

New Dubai all started with the announcement of the first freehold apartments available to foreign investors at the Dubai Marina, which has grown from two solitary towers surrounding by building sites into a bustling new community characterised by luxury apartment blocks and many new hotels, restaurants and bars.

Classic is an apt description for this annual stop on the European tour. The finest golfers in the world make the trip to Dubai every year for this $2.5 million tournament, which has crowned past champions such as Ernie Els (above), Tiger Woods, Fred Couples, Seve Ballesteros, Colin Montgomerie (right), José Maria Olazabal, Mark O'Meara, and Eamonn Darcy. Over the years, the Desert Classic has become an important part of the Dubai social season and a must-attend event for the area's growing legion of golfers.

The Dubai Tennis Championships (the biggest event in the Middle East's tennis calendar) attracts the world's best players every year. Roger Federer, Rafael Nadal, Lindsay Davenport and the Williams sisters have all battled it out in Dubai for the coveted title and substantial prize money. Since it was first held in 1993, this highly anticipated event has been staged at the impressive Dubai Tennis Stadium. Great facilities, perfect weather and the chance to get up close to some of the sport's biggest names ensure that the event is always a success.

Before scuba diving became one of Dubai's most popular pastimes, divers of a different sort made their living through the dangerous art of pearl diving. This and other examples of Dubai's rich maritime history are highlighted at the Heritage & Diving Village, along with other traditional crafts. A visit is especially rewarding during holidays and the Dubai Shopping Festival, when the village is host to special events such as traditional weddings, cooking demonstrations and other examples of Dubai's cultural wealth.

Painted entirely in vibrant yellow, red and blue, and set within the beautiful surroundings of Creekside Park, the colourful Children's City building is hard to miss. It's a one-stop venue for inquisitive minds – there's a Planetarium focusing on the solar system and space exploration, a Nature Centre for information on land and sea environments, and the Discovery Space, which reveals the miracles and mysteries of the human body. The interactive environment teaches children thousands of interesting facts, the most important being that learning can be fun.

Dubai is blessed with one of the world's most enticing coastlines. From immaculate white sand to the gentle azure sea, the many public and private beaches attract visitors and residents alike. With so much unspoilt shoreline to choose from, Dubai's beaches never seem overcrowded, and an evening stroll is the perfect way to experience the tranquility of the Arabian Gulf.

Kitesurfing involves holding a really, really big kite while riding a surfboard fastened to the feet. This fast, exciting, physically demanding sport has become very popular in Dubai, where conditions are perfect. For parasailing on the other hand, you don't require as much athletic skill – just the pure courage to strap on a parachute, get hooked up to a speedboat, and glide through the air at great height. It's an exhilarating ride offering unique views of Dubai's coast, the Palm Jumeirah and The World projects, and the turquoise waters of the Gulf.

Considering that Dubai grew out of desert, visitors may be surprised by the many lush and lovingly tended green areas around the city. There are numerous beautiful parks, all offering shaded picnic areas, playgrounds and expansive lawns. Certain parks have boating lakes or walking tracks as additional features. Jumeira Beach Park and Al Mamzar Beach Park combine traditional park greenery with pristine sandy beaches, complete with mature palm trees that provide some welcome shelter from the sun.

A walk along the Deira creekside dhow wharfage provides
a fascinating glimpse of Dubai as a working city, where the
primitive dhows are often moored eight, nine and even ten
abreast. Vessels from Iran, India and other distant lands can
be seen loading and unloading everything from spices and
textiles to refrigerators and used cars, and because only
traditional wooden dhows are allowed to enter, the creek still
has the feel of an old-world trading port.

Dubai is widely regarded as the shopping capital of the Middle East, and with good reason. The city is home to a growing number of world-class malls, stocking everything from local treasures to international brands and designer labels. Deira City Centre, Wafi City, Mall of the Emirates, Souk Madinat Jumeirah and the BurJuman Centre all compete for the attention of Dubai's eager shoppers, and Dubai Mall (scheduled to open in late 2008) is set to become the biggest shopping mall on the planet.

Al Qasr is described as the 'palace' at the heart of the beachfront Madinat Jumeirah Resort. Surrounded by a system of waterways to form its own island, this five-star grand boutique hotel is home to almost 300 rooms and suites offering the ultimate in luxury and Arabic hospitality. For guests who really want to get away from it all, the Dar Al Masyaf summer-houses provide beach or waterfront seclusion with the same levels of comfort and opulence.

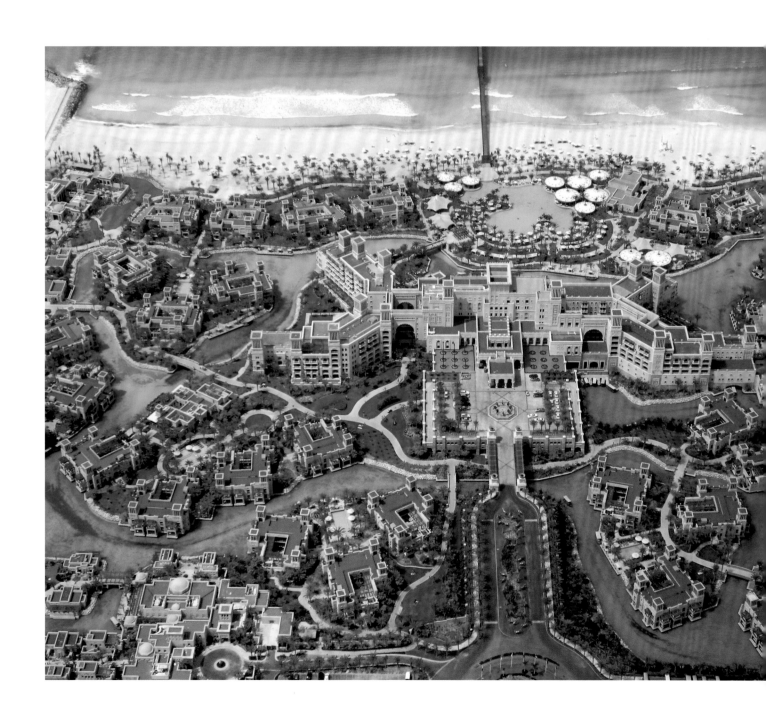

When the temperature rises and you need to cool off, spend a few hours of watery fun at the Wild Wadi water park next to the Jumeirah Beach Hotel. This aqua wonderland has 23 rides to suit all ages and bravery levels – meet fellow thrill-seekers at the top of the Jumeirah Sceirah, the tallest, fastest, freefall waterslide outside North America, or try the rather more sedate Juha's Journey, a relaxing voyage along meandering waterways.

With all the attention being paid to Dubai's rapid growth, it is easy to overlook the UAE's long tradition of Islamic devotion. But the regular call to prayer from the minarets of the majestic Jumeira Mosque (and the hundreds of other mosques around the city) reminds visitors that Dubai's history and culture is fundamentally shaped by Islam. The older generation has witnessed almost unimaginable change, and many have fascinating stories to tell about the past. While modern machines and inventions transformed daily living for Dubai's residents, locals are determined that the old way of life will not be forgotten.

With Dubai's dizzying growth, an increase in traffic congestion is to be expected. The massive interchanges on Sheikh Zayed Road work to keep the traffic flowing, but are also meticulously landscaped and add to the city's aesthetic appeal. A small army of dedicated workers ensures that these interchanges are not merely road junctions, but lush gardens beside the highway.

The exquisite steel and glass Emirates Towers are a central landmark for the people of Dubai, housing numerous offices, a luxury hotel, upmarket shopping, and restaurants and bars – some of which have the best views in (and of) the city. As you walk beneath them, you'll understand the bold statement their creators were making about Dubai's growing prominence as a place of innovation and sophistication. Their height may soon be passed, but they will always serve as a reminder of Dubai's unbridled sprint towards modernity at the beginning of the new millennium.

Horses! Hats! Celebrities! More Hats! The world's richest horserace is also the apex of the city's social calendar. Every year Dubai gets dressed up and rubs shoulders with the world's beautiful people. The occasional black tie is not uncommon, and milliners everywhere dream of such a party. This truly stunning event also attracts the finest, fastest horses in the world. The Dubai World Cup is a fitting tribute to the Arabian love of majestic horses, and the best party you'll find in Dubai all year.

Bastakiya offers a wealth of sights, sounds, smells and tastes just waiting to be discovered. After exploring the area on foot, take time to sit, relax, and soak up the atmosphere at one of the many street-front restaurants and cafés. As you enjoy a delicious Arabic meal surrounded by ancient buildings and windtowers, with the evening call to prayer echoing through the narrow streets, you cannot help but imagine what life was like in Dubai many generations ago.

Whether it's a romantic date, a get-together with friends and family, or an office party, a dinner cruise along the creek is the perfect setting. If you set sail late in the afternoon you'll be rewarded with an unforgettable sunset, with warm light reflecting off modern buildings along the creek. Vessels vary from luxurious glass and chrome cruisers to the more humble, traditional wooden dhow. Passengers can enjoy fine food and vibrant entertainment, before settling into a comfortable majlis with a fragrant shisha pipe to watch the creekside sights glide by.

The traditional dhows which line the creek and can be seen sailing along Dubai's coastline are strikingly similar to the old boats which served the region in past centuries. Dhow-building yards are a fascinating place where visitors can view dhows being built in a manner passed from generation to generation. These huge boats, still constructed one at a time by hand, are an interesting reminder of what has made Dubai the commercial capital that it is today.

As a city speeding towards the future, it makes sense that Dubai should have a world-class motor racing circuit. With various track configurations, including a 5.39km Grand Prix circuit, the Autodrome hosts a variety of races throughout the year. The grandstand seats almost 7,000 spectators, and a business park built around the circuit provides the ideal location for the motor racing and automotive industries.

For all of the beauty, isolation and serenity the open desert offers, one of its greatest attractions is the thrill factor of the undulating dunes. Whether your vehicle of choice is a 4WD, a desert buggy or a quad bike, once you're in the desert you can just turn the key, unleash the horsepower and tackle the terrain. The endless open spaces are a playground for off-road enthusiasts – one which is ever-changing and always available.

The creek (also known by its Arabic name 'Al Khor') divides the city in two – the older Deira side, and the newer Bur Dubai side. Apart from being a busy trading hub, the creek is also an important cultural and tourism hotspot. Starting from the historic house of Sheikh Rashid, winding through Deira's modern skyline and traditional dhow wharfages, and ending at the Khor Dubai Wildlife Sanctuary, the creek epitomises the merging of past, present and future.

Dubai's creek developed as a safe port for the trading of pearls, fish, gold and other goods offloaded from larger ships offshore. As the city grew, Sheikh Rashid saw the creek's potential and ordered its expansion, allowing these larger boats to enter. Scores of traditional wooden dhows can still be seen carrying on their trade as they have for generations, in stark contrast to the modern residential and office towers that now line the banks of the creek.

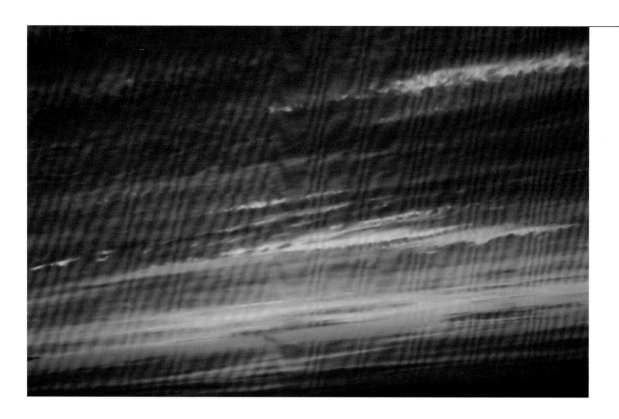

Golden sand, crystal clear water, and year-round good weather make a day of sunbathing and swimming, or an evening's barbecue, an excellent option for those who might need to remind themselves of Dubai's simpler pleasures. For all of the city's attractions and distractions, the one thing that sets it apart from many others is mile upon mile of beautiful beach. From the popular beach park at Al Mamzar to the secluded Jebel Ali coastline, Dubai is full of places where you can recharge your batteries by simply digging your toes into the sand.

Despite marching full-speed into the future, Dubai has a fascinating cultural heritage. Displays of traditional music and dancing are often seen, and the younger generation are just as willing to participate as their elders. A popular dance is the Ayyala, where two rows of men face each other to simulate a battle between tribes. Accompanied by a rhythmic drumbeat, the men wave their long sticks and sway back and forth to signify victories and defeats in the battle, while each row takes it in turn to sing lines that taunt and challenge the opposition.

Dubai has much to offer, from beaches and desert to graceful architecture and modern shopping. But perhaps one of its greatest assets is its reputation as a culinary paradise. Whether you choose atmospheric gourmet, relaxed alfresco, or a roadside shawarma, you'll seldom have a bad meal in Dubai. Mirroring the city's eclectic cultural mix, just about every cuisine in the world is represented, from Arabic and Indian to Mexican and Vietnamese. Each season brings with it a fresh crop of innovative chefs who keep Dubai's culinary scene on a par with any of the world's great cities.

Standing in stark contrast to the sprawling desert, the UAE's
mountains, most notably the Eastern Hajar range, are home
to a surprising array of flora and fauna, and provide some of
the most spectacular views in the Emirates. The arid limestone
cliffs, crags, peaks and wadis, breathtaking in their scale and
density, attract climbers, hikers, off-road drivers and campers,
all looking for a quiet respite from the city.

The Dubai Shopping Festival is an extremely busy and exciting month for Dubai's residents and visitors, as the city is decked out in its finest party lights and decorations. Shops around the city offer monumental discounts and prizes of cars, money and gold. A lavish opening ceremony begins a month of fireworks and celebrations, most notably at Global Village, a collection of fairground rides and themed pavilions selling crafts, food, and artefacts from countries all over the world. During the festival, the city hosts daily cultural and entertainment events for the whole family.

Though it is in many ways a harsh environment, the desert is also a place of deep serenity and quiet beauty. The landscape may initially appear forbidding, but visitors to Dubai often discover that a foray into the desert ends up being the highlight of their trip. A few minutes into the vast emptiness gives one the feeling of complete solitude, where the silence is pervasive and the beauty inspiring.

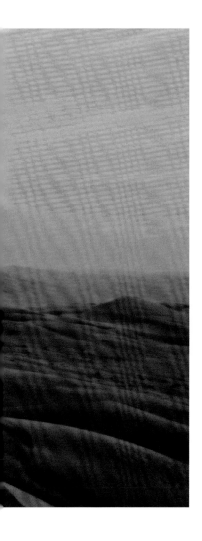

Sensory overload is part of the Dubai experience, but nowhere do sights, sounds, smells and tastes come together like at the old spice souk. Endless open sacks containing spices, herbs, dried fruits and nuts spill out of the small shops onto the pavement. A trip into the heart of this traditional Arabian market transports the visitor to a bygone era, making it easy to forget the modern metropolis that Dubai has become.

Dubai is often referred to as the 'City of Gold', not least because it has one of the best gold markets in the world. A walk through this old souk is a dazzling experience – narrow streets are lined with gold dealers, their shop windows bursting with gold and diamonds. A closer look reveals some unique pieces of jewellery, created expertly by craftsmen and priced according to weight. It's a great place to get souvenirs, and part of the pleasure is bargaining with the shopkeepers for a good deal.

It was not long ago that the truly dedicated made their way around Dubai's only golf course, with sand putting surfaces referred to as 'browns' instead of 'greens'. From these humble beginnings the emirate has come a long way, and visitors now have a host of world-class courses to choose from. Designed by the likes of Greg Norman, Robert Trent Jones II and Colin Montgomerie, these oases in the desert, along with virtually guaranteed good weather and hospitality that no other location can match, have made Dubai one of the world's premier golfing destinations.

Offering a fascinating glimpse into the region's past and dramatic development, the Dubai Museum is well worth a visit for tourists and residents alike. Creative exhibits highlight Dubai's military, commercial and cultural history, showing what life was like before the discovery of oil and the subsequent modernisation. Visitors can learn about the importance of the creek, dhow construction, traditional architecture, the desert, pearl diving, mosques and souks. Some of the museum's artefacts date back 4,000 years. It is found in Al Fahedi Fort, which is believed to be the city's oldest building.

Sitting side by side on the banks of the creek are two of Deira's most distinctive buildings – the headquarters of the Dubai Chamber of Commerce and Industry, and Carlos Ott's magnificent mirror-fronted National Bank of Dubai building. While both are home to a world of high finance and corporate deals, they witness the constant crossing of abras and the comings and goings of wooden dhows, echoing a time and a way of life that could have known nothing of the modern developments to come.

Historically, Bedouins valued horses for their speed and stamina, and as symbols of class and wealth. Today, local people still show an obvious passion for their majestic Arabian thoroughbreds. Dubai's ruling family is actively involved in many equestrian sports – Sheikh Mohammed himself is a formidable competitor in endurance riding, where the limits of horse and rider are tested over distances often exceeding a hundred kilometres. The Maktoum family also owns the Godolphin racing team, which enjoys regular success in horse racing events around the world.

As a successful method of adding meat to the diet (most often hare or houbara bustard), the use of falcons for hunting was an integral part of the Bedouin way of life. Today falconry is enthusiastically practised, but just for sport, and it provides a fascinating reminder of the region's past. These magnificent creatures of prey are highly prized and usually very valuable, with the finest birds changing hands for many thousands of dirhams.

From the high-rise buildings that line Sheikh Zayed Road to the majestic Burj Al Arab hotel many miles in the distance, Dubai today is a tribute to hard work, ambition and belief. What was not too long ago a little-known town with few modern amenities is now a vibrant, dynamic and cosmopolitan city that continues to grow at an astonishing pace. Dubai's skyline is destined to maintain its dramatic pace of change as future generations push the city's evolution even further.

FACTS & FIGURES

Geography

Dubai is the second largest of the seven emirates that make up the United Arab Emirates (UAE). The others are Abu Dhabi, Ajman, Fujairah, Ras Al Khaimah, Sharjah and Umm Al Quwain. The UAE is situated on the north-eastern part of the Arabian Peninsula, sharing borders with Saudi Arabia and Oman, and has coasts on both the Arabian Gulf and the Gulf of Oman. The total area of the UAE is around 83,000 square kilometres, most of which lies in Abu Dhabi. Inland, the country consists of salt flats (sabkha), gravel plains, vast expanses of desert, and the Hajar Mountains to the east. The emirate of Dubai occupies 3,885 square kilometres, with a coastline on the Arabian Gulf.

Population

The population of the UAE is an estimated 4,400,000, with around 1,400,000 people living in Dubai. Emirati 'Nationals' account for only 20% of this figure, with the remaining 80% consisting of expatriate workers, mainly from the Indian Subcontinent, Asia, other Arab countries and Europe.

Rulers

The Ruler of Dubai is Sheikh Mohammed bin Rashid Al Maktoum, who is also the Vice President and Prime Minister of the UAE, and is considered the driving force behind Dubai's phenomenal development. His brother Sheikh Hamdan bin Rashid Al Maktoum is the UAE Minister of Finance and Industry.

Economy

Dubai has one of the fastest-growing economies in the world, and while oil was important to its development, it contributes less than 6% to Dubai's GDP. The major contributors to the economy are transport and travel, construction, real estate, trade and manufacturing, financial services, telecommunications, and leisure and tourism.

Currency

The monetary unit of Dubai and the UAE is the dirham (abbreviated to Dhs. or AED). One dirham is divided into 100 fils. Banknotes come in denominations of Dhs.5, Dhs.10, Dhs.20, Dhs.50, Dhs.100, Dhs.200, Dhs.500 and Dhs.1000. Coins are 1 fil, 5 fils, 10 fils, 25 fils, 50 fils and Dhs.1. The 1, 5 and 10 fil coins are rarely used so you may not always receive the exact change. The dirham is pegged to the US dollar at a rate of Dhs.3.67 to US$1.

Climate

Dubai has a sub-tropical, arid climate, with blue skies and high temperatures most of the year. Rainfall is infrequent, falling mainly in winter (November to March). Temperatures range from a low of around 10°C (50°F) in winter, to a high of 48°C (118°F) in summer. The high temperatures and humidity in the summer months can make it uncomfortable to be outdoors for long periods, but all hotels, restaurants, entertainment venues and shopping malls have air conditioning.

Local Time

The United Arab Emirates is four hours ahead of UTC (Universal Coordinated Time – formerly known as GMT). There is no daylight saving time.

Electricity

The electricity supply in Dubai is 220/240 volts at 50 cycles. The socket type is the same as the three-pin British system.

Visas

Visa requirements for entering Dubai vary greatly between different nationalities, and regulations should always be checked before travelling, since details can change with little or no warning.

All visitors, except citizens of GCC countries (Bahrain, Kuwait, Qatar, Oman, Saudi Arabia and UAE), require a visa. However, citizens of the countries listed below automatically get a visit visa stamp in their passport upon arrival, which is usually valid for 60 days.

Visit Visa on Arrival

Andorra, Australia, Austria, Belgium, Brunei, Canada, Cyprus, Denmark, Finland, France, Germany, Greece, Hong Kong, Iceland, Ireland, Italy, Japan, Liechtenstein, Luxembourg, Malaysia, Malta, Monaco, The Netherlands, New Zealand, Norway, Portugal, San Marino, Singapore, South Korea, Spain, Sweden, Switzerland, United Kingdom, United States of America and Vatican City.

Other nationalities may be able to obtain a 30 day tourist visa sponsored by a local hotel or tour operator prior to arrival, while for visitors travelling onwards to another destination, a transit visa (up to 96 hours) can be arranged through the airline.

Religion

Islam is the official religion of Dubai and the UAE, although other religions such as Christianity and Hinduism are respected.

Drinking Water

The tap water is purified and safe to drink, but people may prefer the taste of locally bottled mineral water, of which there are several available brands.

Dialling Code

The international dialling code to the UAE is +971. The local code for Dubai is 04.

Language

The official language of the UAE is Arabic, but English is widely spoken and almost all public information (road signs, menus) is printed in both languages. Dubai has a diverse population and as a result, many other languages are also heard.

Opening Hours

Some shops open from 09:00 to 13:00 and then from 16:00 to 21:00, and others stay open throughout the day. Malls are usually open from 10:00 to 22:00. On Fridays, shops often open at 14:00, after Friday prayers. Business hours vary between sectors, and the weekend is officially Friday and Saturday.

Dress Code

While the dress code in Dubai is liberal compared to other cities in the region, visitors should respect local customs by dressing modestly. Lightweight clothes are suitable for most of the year, but something slightly warmer may be needed for winter months, and when visiting restaurants, malls or cinemas where air conditioning can be cold.

Dubai

DISCOVERED

EXPLORER
www.explorerpublishing.com